Visualization

The Efficacy Of Visualization: Potent Visualization
Methodologies To Attain Boundless Triumph

*(Simple Meditation Practices With Transformative
Potential)*

Jackie Wilkins

TABLE OF CONTENT

What Is Visualization?

Have you ever pondered upon the concept of visualization? Individuals reach the inference that one must possess literal visions. They perceive it as an attribute exclusive to those deemed holy, yet it is important to note that these visions transcend the boundaries of any particular religious affiliation. The visualizations you experience are deliberate mental constructs that can be vividly perceived within your mind. When employed to influence the course of your life, these visions might encompass mental imagery depicting your envisioned future state, encompassing your desired dwelling place and the desired companions you seek to associate with. These constructs have the capacity to be as intricate as your level of interest allows, or alternatively, they can be surprisingly straightforward. It heavily relies on the specific nature of your pursuit.

Let us endeavor to provide you with an illustration. During my childhood, I envisioned myself pursuing a career as a professional concert pianist. I had a strong desire to pursue that path. Nevertheless, circumstances prevented me from assuming that position. According to my parents, their decision was final and non-negotiable. The conclusion of the narrative seemed imminent, yet my aspirations of becoming a concert pianist were not extinguished solely due to the unfortunate financial predicament that my parents encountered. It stayed within my mind. During a time when fellow children joyfully frolicked in the meadows, I would recline upon the verdant blades, gently shut my eyelids, and envision the resplendent piano and the dulcet melodies it produced. My vision remained present. It was solidified through the power of my own mental imagery. I witnessed the presence of the piano and had the auditory perception of its sounds. I experienced the ambiance generated by the music it emitted. From my perspective, the piano was unquestionably genuine.

In contrast, my sister harbored a desire to pursue the cello. She harbored unfavorable sentiments toward pursuing a career in music. She displayed characteristics of being a challenging adolescent who, out of curiosity, chose to engage with a musical instrument that exceeded the conventional dimensions by twofold. She did not envision herself participating in the activity and was not overly distraught when my parents informed her that they were unable to financially accommodate the instruction. Hence, there was a lack of envisioning and it was highly improbable that she would ever realize that aspiration, given its fleeting nature.

The power of my imagination sustained me during my adolescence, until the opportunity arose for me to financially support those lessons. As I positioned myself before the piano, an undeniable sense of destiny enveloped me, and I became acutely aware that my ability to envisage success not only within my examinations but also in perpetuity, would be profoundly influential.

The aforementioned examples highlight the fact that a vivid mental image was effective in one case, while the absence of such imagery rendered the pursuit of playing the cello futile in the other scenario. The idea lacked sufficient strength and failed to be sustained as a prevailing vision.

Similarly, individuals who engage in regular visualization practices may not be expressing a desire for tangible possessions. They might be envisioning a mental state characterized by serenity amidst turbulence, or a heightened state of consciousness. The regular implementation of visualization, nevertheless, renders these journeys feasible, as opposed to being mere transient aspirations.

To accomplish endeavors in one's life, be they tangible or emotional, it is imperative to possess a clear understanding of the objectives in question, and this is precisely where visualization plays a significant role. In the forthcoming chapters, we will elucidate the utilization of visualization as a means to attain desired objectives in life, simultaneously providing instruction on a structured form of meditation designed to bolster one's pursuit of optimal self-fulfillment. After acquiring proficiency in their usage, they prove to be immensely formidable.

It is not solely a matter of attaining all of your desires. Certain desires that you may harbor momentarily might not align with your long-term aspirations. The human cognitive faculties experience a multitude of fluctuations and fluctuations over the span of an individual's lifespan. Through the implementation of visualization techniques, you have the ability to exert deliberate influence over the direction of your life, optimizing the pursuit of your desired path while minimizing unproductive, aimless pursuits. Many individuals possess vague aspirations that hinder their progress and impede any noticeable advancement. Through the utilization of this particular method of meditation and deliberate visualization, one has the capacity to attain their desired goals and embark upon a pathway towards spiritual enlightenment.

Visualization Exercises

Essential Visualization Exercises for Achieving Success

Your focus determines the objects or circumstances that you draw towards yourself. This statement is indeed accurate, as we exist within an expansive milieu of resonating energy, unbeknownst to us, which greatly influences our cognitive processes and perceptions. The ideas within our existence are endeavoring to articulate themselves throughout the entirety of our existence. These are the underlying factors which drive our creative capabilities, and once we come to recognize their existence, we can embark upon our life journeys with a distinct direction and, above all, a meaningful objective.

With careful introspection, one can ascertain that every action is preceded by a cognitive process, as thoughts serve as the inception point for all endeavors. Prior to speaking or engaging in action, it is imperative to commence by pondering upon the matter at hand. It first springs to life within our imagination.

It is within our capacity to pursue our aspirations, regardless of their level of difficulty, and we can achieve them by virtue of our ability to envision and anticipate forthcoming events with inevitability. Moreover, the greater our capacity to contemplate our aspirations for the future, the higher the likelihood of realizing them.

Definition

"A rudimentary practice of visualization has the potential to yield significant benefits, such as:

Activating the right-hemisphere of your brain

Engaging the prefrontal cortex and amygdala

Enhancing one's creative prowess and ability to concentrate

This fundamental practice will assist you in effectively visualizing images within your mind's eye. If you commence engaging in the exercise, the process of visualizing mental imagery will be effortlessly achievable for you.

We consistently engage in mental imagery, yet a significant number of individuals remain oblivious to this fact. Through the completion of this exercise, our attention can be channeled towards the deliberate formation of desired mental imagery, as opposed to sporadic and spontaneous mental images.

Despite its simplicity, this exercise has the potential to enhance and stimulate your imagination. The primary aim of this activity is to enhance your capacity for profound mental concentration and the ability to single-mindedly focus on a specific object or task. With consistent practice, it will also augment your reserves of visual imagery.

As the refinement of your visualization progresses, a corresponding enhancement will be observed in your two interconnected cognitive abilities. As you enhance your capacity to construct intricate mental visuals, your proficiency exponentially amplifies. The skill of imaginative imagery holds utmost importance in facilitating cognitive enlargement. Devoid of it, envisioning your envisioned future becomes inconceivable, consequently impeding any progress towards its realization. Now that we have gained insight into the genuine power of visualization, let us now advance to the fundamental exercises designed to cultivate one's ability to visualize.

Instructions on Performing the Exercises

1st Exercise

It is imperative that we possess a photograph for the purpose of analysis in this exercise. It is imperative that you direct your attention towards meticulously examining every aspect present in the photograph, committing them to memory. Subsequently, proceed to close your eyes and endeavor to visualize the image within your mental faculties. Please remember all the specific information you have collected, including the depiction of the river, the strikingly clear blue sky, the shade of the roof, and any other elements that are discernible within the image. For a more formal tone: "You may acquire additional information by revisiting the photograph." Persist in the act of mental imagery until the precise depiction materializes within your consciousness. Please be reminded that the purpose of the exercise is not to evaluate you.

2nd Exercise

In contrast to the prior two-dimensional (2D) task, we are elevating it to the subsequent level: the realm of three dimensions (3D). On this occasion, feel free to utilize any diminutive item available. It could potentially be either a pencil or your keychain. Similar to the previous exercise, endeavor to commit to memory every pertinent detail pertaining to the object. However, don't rush. Concentrate on analyzing it. Subsequently, proceed with the act of closing your eyes whilst making a conscious effort to mentally envisage the object. However, the journey does not cease at this juncture. Round 2 presents a somewhat more arduous task. You endeavor to mentally manipulate the orientation of your object. Envision all the intricate facets observable from various perspectives of the object. Endeavor to incorporate imaginative elements, such as the environmental context surrounding the object. Envision your object in a state of repose upon the table, or imagine its ability to cast an independent shadow.

3rd Exercise

This exercise commences from the second exercise, yet elevates the difficulty level, thereby posing a challenge for the majority while a few may perceive it as effortless. In this exercise, you will engage in the cognitive process of envisioning your chosen object, albeit with your eyes unobstructed. Actualize its form within the physical realm by perceiving it as it truly appears. Engage with the object, causing it to rotate or transfer it from one location to another. Strive to seamlessly integrate it with the tangible entities within your surroundings. Envision your item positioned delicately upon your study table, situated atop your bookshelf, or suspended elegantly from the ceiling.

4th Exercise

The exercise is the catalyst for an abundance of enjoyable activities. On this occasion, I encourage you to not only envision the image, but to also immerse yourself within its depiction. Allow your mind to conjure up a tranquil setting. It may be a seaside destination, a cinema, or a boutique café of your choice. Now, mentally imagine the surrounding environment with your presence incorporated. Do not merely consider the visual aspects of the scene; endeavor to immerse yourself within its surroundings.

Please endeavor to recollect your remaining four senses. Are you able to perceive the rhythmic undulations of the ocean waves, the cacophonous calls of avian creatures, or the jovial outbursts amidst the gathering of spectators? Are you able to perceive the tactile sensations of the various objects you come into contact with, such as the moist glass containing juice, the warm coffee mug, or the impending consumption of popcorn? What about your taste? Do you derive pleasure from the act of consuming your chocolate flavored frozen dessert through licking? Are you able to perceive the savory flavor of the popcorn?

Please ensure that you actively engage in envisioning yourself within the scene rather than simply contemplating the scene. Make an effort to enhance the level of intricacy and authenticity in your mental visualization.

5th Exercise

In this ultimate exercise, we shall endeavor to envision aspects that bear greater resemblance to actuality. Contemplate a fresh perspective for the setting utilized in the preceding task. On this occasion, make an effort to engage with it. Engage in light physical activity, manipulate the sand along the shoreline, or assuming a seated position at a local café.

Next, endeavor to involve an additional individual. It has the potential to be either your closest companion or someone you have admired for a significant period of time. Envision engaging in light-hearted banter with a close companion, or engaging in physical affection with someone who captivates your interest. Now, may I inquire about your current state of well-being?

These exercises will further prove advantageous for you due to your active imagination. The practice facilitates the attainment of elevated levels of creative cognition. The process of imagination is a cognitive ability that falls under higher-order thinking, and it elicits activation in the amygdala region of the brain. This will enhance the connectivity to the pre-frontal cortex, resulting in an improved emotional state.

Following the completion of these exercises, it may come to your attention that your cognitive capacity has been augmented, albeit subtly. Your ability to visualize has been enhanced, thereby augmenting your capacity for mastering self-hypnosis. Your proficiency in tasks associated with the right-hemisphere has been significantly heightened, allowing you to competently articulate constructive recommendations.

Upon completion of the five exercises, you will be adequately prepared to engage in the process of creating a mental motion picture. In the film, one is able to envision their potential future— achieving objectives, acquiring new proficiencies, or shedding negative inclinations.

Tips:

Exercise caution in the words you choose to vocalize.

Direct your attention towards the desired outcomes rather than dwelling on undesired ones. It is imperative that you exercise caution and mindfulness when selecting your words. Please refrain from employing words that accurately depict the objects or ideas that you do not genuinely desire. Should you decide to do so, you will inadvertently be drawing towards yourself whatever it is that you wish to avoid attracting. As an illustration, avoid expressing "I don't want to be tardy," but rather state "I aspire to be punctual." Can you observe the disparity in the extent of optimism between the latter statement and the former? An alternative instance entails expressing, "I aspire to attain a state of sound physical and mental well-being" rather than articulating, "I aim to avoid being afflicted with this illness."

Be grateful.

The greater the extent to which you articulate dissatisfaction with your life, the more prone you become to attracting situations and adversities that give rise to further discontent. Cease envisioning the negative aspects of your existence and endeavor to direct your attention towards the positive aspects, expressing gratitude for them.

Returning to step 4, subsequent to concluding the ten-minute visualization exercise and regaining consciousness, commence expressing gratitude for all aspects of your existence, as it aligns with the natural order of things. Demonstrate gratitude for your present abode, as it offers you shelter; for your current occupation, irrespective of its alignment with your aspirations, as it provides sustenance; for the automobile you currently possess; and for the individuals you encounter on your journey. Express gratitude for everything and maintain a positive outlook in your approach. Through expressing gratitude, one has a propensity to draw in additional reasons for gratitude, subsequently nourishing the mind with positive energy. This serves as a powerful mechanism for enhancing visualization.

What Methods Can Be Employed To Access And Harness Our Latent Capabilities Through The Utilization Of Imaginative Visualization?

Construct a comprehensive arrangement of your aspirations or preferences. Mentally envisage them and repeatedly create visualizations of the arrangements. Expend 5 minutes daily in visualizing your desires. The establishment of a consistent practice would greatly enhance the effectiveness of one's visualization efforts. In due course, you can determine the amount of time you are able to allocate towards visualization in order to enhance your situation.

Please allocate that time specifically to mitigate potential distractions and to ensure adequate rest. Seek out a tranquil and pleasant location in which to rest and engage in the aforementioned techniques or methods. The more you visualize your aspirations, the sooner you accomplish them.

At the outset, it is advisable to visualize the possessions you presently possess. It is merely a cognitive strategy and a substantial element of this process. One must adopt the mindset that they already possess the object of their desire. You are obliged to commence living and experience those visualizations.

The partially conscious mind fails to discern the distinction between actuality and fantasy. The subconscious mind will respond to the mental or imaginative constructs that your mind generates, regardless of their current existence or lack thereof.

Use your all senses. Envision yourself attaining the objective you seek. Observing from the same corporeal vessel in which you currently reside and perceiving through your own ocular organs, one would undoubtedly discern that the act of visualizing possesses a considerably greater potency compared to mere imaginative cognizance. Enhance your imaginative abilities by engaging in additional practice, as the more realistic your visualizations become, the higher the efficacy of your efforts will be. Aspire to great heights and derive maximum enjoyment through its actualization.

Envision a cinematic experience, embellishing it with intricate storylines and vivid imagery. Engage in the playing of ambient music and derive enjoyment from its immersive nature.

It is advisable to manifest your desire through physical action. Examine all possible scenarios regarding the circumstances preceding and subsequent to the achievement of your objective.

You ought to derive satisfaction from your capacity for imaginative visualization and the moments you dedicate to it. Ensure that the occasion is a pleasant and serene gathering for you. At your convenience, you may choose to recline momentarily and devote the ensuing tranquility to the practice of imaginative visualization, wherein you envision the realization of your aspirations. This will provide you with additional assistance.

Enhance The Visual Appeal Of Your Charts

This Chapter Is Centered On Consolidating The Entirety Of The Acquired Information Thus Far. Take Into Account All The Knowledge You Have Acquired Regarding Vision, Perception, Pre-Attentive Characteristics, Elements And Principles Of Design, As Well As Principles Of Layout. Integrate Them Within Your Design, Upholding The Cohesive Narrative And Aesthetic Elements Of The Overall Visual Composition.

However, Does The Significance Of Aesthetics Outweigh That Of Functional Design? I Think So, Yes. The Initial Formation Of A Viewer's Overall Perception Occurs Immediately Prior To Further Investigation. Individuals Generally Have A Natural Inclination Towards Objects Of Beauty, And The Presence Of Attractive Aesthetics Renders Visual Content More Visually Appealing, Thereby Attracting A Diverse Array Of

Viewers And Ensuring A Positive User Experience. The Visual Component Of A Design Has The Potential To Elicit A Specific Ambiance, Concept, Sentiment, Or Sensation Among The Viewers. Moreover, Individuals Exhibit Heightened Levels Of Patience, Dependability, And Clemency When Confronted With An Aesthetically Pleasing Design.

Designing A Data Visualization Is A Fulfilling Yet Arduous Undertaking That Compresses Extensive Amounts Of Data Into A Single Frame. By Enhancing Its Visual Appeal And Creating A Lasting Impression In The Minds Of The Audience, You Can Prompt Them To Pause, Observe, And Delve Further Into The Subject Matter.

How To Guarantee That Your Design Exhibits A Visually Appealing Aesthetic.

As Eloquently Expressed By The Esteemed Architect And Designer Mies Van Der Rohe, The Concept Of "Less Is More" Holds Profound Significance. Envision Your Prospective Design As An

Empty Canvas Or Pristine Screen, Awaiting The Grace Of Your Creative Touch. Each Additional Element That Is Introduced Onto The Canvas Becomes An Additional Element That Requires Cognitive Processing By The Viewer. Hence, It Is Imperative That We Delve Into The Core Of Our Storytelling And Center Our Design On Minimalism, With A Particular Emphasis On Catering To Our Audience. Consider Reflecting Upon The Essential Elements Necessary For The Visual Representation In Order To Effectively Communicate Your Data Narrative, Ensuring That The User Obtains Sufficient Contextual Understanding. It Is Important To Bear In Mind That The Cognitive Capabilities Of Your Audience Are Finite, And Therefore It Is Incumbent Upon You To Carefully And Strategically Craft Your Design. Regard Your Completed Data Visualization As A Forthcoming Journey That Necessitates Preparation. You Are Limited To Bringing Only A Compact Case To Accommodate Your Essential Belongings. What Items Are Typically Stored Within The Case?

Think Like A Minimalist

However, What Criteria Do You Employ In Determining The Selection Of Data To Retain? Regrettably, A Definitive Response Cannot Be Provided As The Creation Of Data Visualizations Caters To A Multitude Of Scenarios And Target Audiences. However, A Fundamental Principle That We Have Discussed, Which Holds Utmost Significance In Minimizing Cognitive Load, Is To Decrease Visual Clutter. Clutter Pertains To Visual Elements That Occupy Space But Do Not Contribute To Comprehension. They Have The Capacity To Render A Data Visualization As Overly Intricate As It Truly Is Not, Thereby Deterring The Audience From Engaging With Your Design. Please Be Cognizant Of The Fact That Our Working Memory Has A Capacity To Process 4-5 Clusters Of Information Before It Becomes Strained And Requires Additional Effort To Comprehend. Crafting A Straightforward And Uncluttered Design Will Effectively Convey A Clear Message

To Your Audience And Establish An Immediate Connection With Them.

Recall The Earlier Discussion Pertaining To The Principles Of Gestalt. When Endeavoring To Differentiate Between The Fundamental Components And Extraneous Elements, Take Into Account Concepts Of Closure, Continuity, Connection, Proximity, And Repetition During The Process Of Your Design. In Addition, You May Enhance The Visual Appeal By Employing Alternative Methods To Declutter And Draw Focus, Such As:

Eliminating Superfluous Elements Such As Grid Lines, Borders, And Underlines.

Establishing Visual Contrast Through The Application Of Contrasting Colors, Such As White, To Outline Shapes.

Minimizing The Quantity Of Colors Utilized In The Design Or Adhering To A Restricted Color Scheme.

Employing Symbols Or Motifs In Lieu Of Hues Or Shades

Devise A Monochromatic Strategy Before Incorporating Vibrant Elements, If Desired.

Employing Negative Space As A Means To Accentuate Or Juxtapose, Instead Of Perceiving It As Vacant Space.

Organize For Efficiency

The Preceding Chapters Have Addressed Techniques For Conceptualizing And Organizing One's Thoughts, As Well As Emphasized Strategies For Drawing Viewers' Focus To Key Elements Within A Design Through Approaches Such As The Gestalt Principles And Pre-Attentive Attributes. Pre-Attentive Characteristics Have The Ability To Communicate To The Observer The Focal Points And Subsequent Directions Of Attention. Utilizing These Characteristics Guarantees That Each Element Is Given Adequate Prominence On The Page, Minimizing Excessive Competition.

Utilizing Various Techniques Can Indicate Significance, Nonetheless, The Prevailing Strategy Entails Employing Color As A

Means Of Emphasizing. Emphasizing The Component Through The Application Of A Distinct Color Or Font Serves To Draw Attention To That Particular Element. The Utilization Of Highlighting In This Manner Delivers A Distinct Visual Indication Of The Primary Focus Area, Albeit Contingent Upon The Reduction Of Clutter Present On The Page. Failure To Identify And Eliminate Distractions Will Result In A Visually Disorienting Experience. Outlined Below Are Several Factors Worth Considering, As They Can Assist You In Identifying These Distractions And Subsequently Enable You To Eliminate Them From Your Design.

The Importance Of Data Varies Among Different Elements. Develop A Comprehensive Outline Delineating The Essential Elements Of Your Narrative, Discarding Any Superfluous Details.

Develop The Ability To Condense Information When Excessive Specificity Is Unnecessary.

Examine Every Component Meticulously And Inquire Whether It Is Indispensable.

What Is The Role It Serves Within The Visual Presentation?

Place Nonessential Information In The Periphery. It Is Advisable To Refrain From Succumbing To The Temptation Of Consolidating All Of Your Work Into One Visual Representation, Particularly If It Lacks A Meaningful Purpose.

Use Visual Hierarchy

Visual Hierarchy Serves As A Mechanism To Effectively Communicate To The Audience The Intended Sequence And Reading Flow Of The Page. This Task Can Be Accomplished By Employing Pre-Attentive Attributes, As Previously Examined In Earlier Sections. By Employing These Distinctive Qualities Of Varying Intensities, You Can Guide The Observer Through Your Visual Composition According To Your Intended Vision. Visual Hierarchy Aims To Leverage The Mechanisms Of Our Sensory Memory. Please Keep In Mind That Sensory Memory Operates Involuntarily And Without Conscious Awareness. An Observer Possesses The Ability To Examine A Page And Detect A Disruption

In A Design, Even In The Absence Of Intentional Scrutiny. The Human Brain Possesses The Innate Ability To Discern Variations In Patterns Without Consciously Engaging In Deliberate Search Or Decision-Making Processes. Our Visual Attention Is Naturally Drawn To The Juxtaposition Of Large Versus. Small, Dark Vs. Light, And Color Vs. No Color. By Capitalizing On These Qualities, We Can Construct A More Cohesive Narrative Within Our Visualization.

Meditation and Visualization

The practice of meditation serves as an initial step towards expanding one's consciousness and acquiring the skill of engaging in the art of creative visualization. Please bear in mind that initial difficulties in meditation should not be a cause for concern. It is natural to require some time to adapt to this novel practice and discover one's genuine appreciation for it. Continue diligently pursuing it, so as to inch closer towards attaining your ultimate objective of harnessing creative visualization to realize all your aspirations in life.

One of the initial aspects to prioritize when embarking on an exploration of creative visualization techniques encompasses diverse modalities of meditation. If you have never delved into any form of meditation techniques, it may appear to be a bewildering and intricate undertaking. Furthermore, it may elude your notice that there exist multiple approaches at your disposal, each with the potential to align with your individual preferences. Your cognitive faculties are equally distinctive as your overall self, thus it is imperative that you thoroughly examine all available alternatives and subsequently determine the option that is most suitable for you. Let us examine a range of diverse meditation methods that can initiate your journey towards self-exploration.

Get Comfortable

Please kindly remove your shoes and ensure that you are not donning any tightly fitted apparel, as this may impede your freedom of movement. When one begins the endeavor of directing their thoughts towards concentration, it is common for the discomfort of one's attire to become the paramount concern. It is crucial to ensure that one's physical hunger has been satiated and that the consumption of a substantial meal has not recently taken place, so as to preempt any additional sources of diversion. With increased practice, one will acquire the ability to engage in meditation regardless of external circumstances. However, in the initial stages, it is advisable to strive for a more effortless meditative experience.

Get Ready

Please make certain that you have a suitable environment conducive to the practice of meditation. You may encounter difficulties in attaining a state of deep relaxation where you transition into sleep, as professionals further suggest that adopting a seated posture can enhance the likelihood of achieving the desired outcome. However, since it is a highly individualized journey, it ultimately hinges on identifying the most conducive circumstances for effecting a transformation in one's state of existence. It is advisable to dim or extinguish the lights and ensure optimal personal comfort in the chosen location.

Be Relaxed

Maintain an upright and erect posture, ensuring that your spine is aligned; envision the crown of your head elongating your back in a vertical manner. Close your eyes and initiate relaxation of each individual part of your body, gradually and systematically. Commence at the lower extremities and ascend, directing attention to each individual muscle and articulation. Proceed with ascending your entire physique, ensuring not to neglect your head and facial region.

Remove Distractions

To attain mental clarity and direct your cognitive processes, it is imperative to minimize extraneous factors that cause diversion and deter your concentration. Please switch off your mobile device to prevent any disruptions. If you desire to incorporate a compact disc or any other facilitator for meditation, it is imperative to ensure its proper arrangement. However, it is worth noting that such aids are not indispensable for the realization of your objectives in the practice of meditation. Furthermore, this practice has the potential to diminish your faculties, as you may become overly reliant on such aids and struggle to achieve a trance state without their presence in the background.

Breathe deeply

Please assume a tranquil posture and direct your attention exclusively to your respiration.

41

Direct your focus towards the sensations experienced while inhaling the air into your lungs and subsequently exhaling it through your oral cavity.

Empty Your Thoughts

By directing your attention solely towards the mantra and your breath, you will effectively dispel thoughts from your mind. Do not be concerned if it requires some time for you to become accustomed to the routine; honing these skills will necessitate some repetition.

Finishing

Once you have completed your meditation and are prepared to return to the realm of the physical, commence a gradual countdown from the number five, ensuring that your eyes remain gently closed. Regain a state of physical awareness gradually and proceed to open your eyes. Make an effort to enhance your meditation abilities through brief sessions, prioritizing quality over quantity. It is advisable to contemplate initiating 5 minute sessions twice daily, gradually increasing the duration thereafter.

Furthermore, aside from this primary approach to meditation, there exist various alternative means by which one can attain the desired state of mind. Consequently, let us explore a few additional options.

Always Focus on Breathing

The initial approach to consider involves directing your attention towards regulating your breath in order to enter a state of meditation. This represents one of the fundamental techniques that will be examined.

Locate a suitable seating arrangement on the floor, a chair, or a cushion in a serene and tranquil environment.

Please shut your eyes and lightly place your tongue against the roof of your mouth. Inhale exclusively through your nostrils while keeping your mouth shut.

Take a deep inhalation through your nasal passages, allowing the air to gradually fill your abdominal region. Subsequently, engage in a full exhalation by gradually expelling the air from your mouth, which should be slightly ajar. Maintain your attention solely on your breath as you continue the process of inhaling and exhaling.

Do not dwell on your breathing; instead, concentrate on clearing your mind entirely.

Walking Meditation

Additionally, you have the opportunity to engage in walking meditation. In this particular modality of meditation, the emphasis is placed on directing one's attention towards the feet instead of focusing on the breath. There exists a myriad of diverse approaches through which one can achieve a state of meditation. These three alternatives are only initial choices, and should they prove effective for you, you may choose to either continue with them or pursue other options.

While moving, direct your attention solely towards the action of placing your foot upon the surface.

Do not permit your gaze or thoughts to stray from your intended concentration.

Maintain your gaze fixed ahead and persevere in directing your attention towards each subsequent stride as you proceed.

Visualizing During The Day

It is crucial to bear in mind that you possess the agency to actualize favorable transformations in your life. A recent study, encompassing multiple cohorts of athletes, revealed that the group which incorporated an equal amount of time into their training regimen for visualization, in addition to their normal practice, exhibited superior performance compared to groups allocating minimal or no time to this cognitive exercise. These findings are expected to demonstrate that you can indeed achieve your objectives by employing identical methodologies. When engaging in self-directed goal reinforcement throughout the course of the day, there exist several supplementary measures that may prove beneficial.

Tell Yourself

Maintain a constant presence of your aspirations for success in your thoughts. While showering in the morning, dedicate your time to indulging in pleasant daydreams involving them. When preparing oneself in front of the mirror, articulate the phrases audibly. Reiterate them audibly while inside the vehicle. Incorporate these visualizations into your daily activities consistently.

Write Them Down

The written language holds significant influence over a considerable number of individuals. Please document your desired outcomes precisely and review them periodically whenever you perceive them slipping away. Keep expanding on it in your journal and enjoy your elaborations on it. Additionally, this can enhance your specific periods dedicated to creative visualization by providing you with heightened concentration for contemplation.

Make a Board

If you encounter an image or text that strikingly resonates with the aspirations you are diligently pursuing, it is advisable to preserve it. Create a tangible vision board by gathering all of these elements to better channel your energy. The clear vision of one's goals can serve as a powerful motivator, driving individuals to exert greater effort in their pursuit of success. This offers a comprehensive visual representation for you to concentrate on, enhancing the sensation that your dreams are readily attainable. Engaging in this practice also serves as a continuous reminder to uphold a positive mindset and to remain receptive to potential opportunities that may have otherwise gone unnoticed.

Data Mining Architecture

Now that you have gained a fundamental understanding of data mining, it is time to delve deeper into the intricacies of the data mining architecture. Key elements of data mining include the data mining engine, data source, pattern evaluation module, knowledge base, data warehouse servers, and graphical user interface. Let us now proceed to examine each of these components in greater depth.

Data Source

Data can be obtained from the following sources:

Database

Data warehouse

Internet

Text files

In order to extract valuable insights through the process of data mining, it is crucial to amass extensive amounts of historical data. The majority of organizations maintain their data within data warehouses or databases. A data warehouse can encompass multiple databases, a repository of data, or spreadsheets in text file format. Alternatively, spreadsheets or text files can serve as suitable sources as they have the capability to encompass certain sets of information.

Different Processes

Prior to transferring the gathered data or information into a data warehouse or database, it is imperative to undertake a series of procedures, including processing, selecting, integrating, and cleansing the information. Due to the aggregation of data from diverse sources with varying data formats, the direct utilization of said information for data mining purposes is not feasible. The utilization of unstructured data in the data mining process will lead to erroneous and deficient outcomes. Hence, the initial phase of the procedure involves cleansing the data that necessitates processing, subsequent to which it is transmitted to the server. The task of data cleansing proves to be more challenging than initially perceived. Various operations can be executed on the data during the process of cleaning, integration, and selection.

Server or Database used for the Storage of Data in a Data Warehouse

After acquiring the desired data from various sources, it can be subjected to cleansing processes before being forwarded to the data warehouse server or database. This serves as the primary data source that will undergo processing and utilization within the data mining process. The individual avails themselves of the server, referring to either yourself or the business, in order to access the pertinent information pertaining to the data mining inquiry.

Data Mining Engine

This component holds significant value within the structure of the data mining architecture, as it encompasses diverse modules that can be employed to execute a range of data mining tasks. These include:

Classification

Characterization

Association

Prediction

Clustering

Time-series analysis

Put simply, it can be stated that this engine serves as the fundamental cornerstone of the entire architecture. The engine encompasses a variety of software and instrumentation designed to extract knowledge and glean insights from the data generated during the mining process. Additionally, the engine can be utilized to acquire further knowledge concerning any type of data that is stored within the server.

Pattern Evaluation Module

This particular model is utilized within the context of data mining architecture to quantify or scrutinize the pattern that variables adhere to, contingent upon a predefined threshold value. This module collaborates with the data mining engine to discern a multitude of patterns within the dataset. The pattern evaluation module utilizes diverse stake measures which collaborate with various data mining modules within the engine to discern distinct patterns or trends present in the datasets. This module employs a stake threshold in order to identify potential concealed patterns and trends within the dataset.

The pattern evaluation module has the capability to collaborate with the mining module, provided that it relies on distinct techniques incorporated in the data mining engine. In order to cultivate proficient and precise data mining models, it is imperative to prioritize the integration of this stake measure's assessment extensively within the mining process. This will guarantee that the model exclusively analyzes the distinct patterns in the dataset.

Graphical User Interface (GUI) " "Graphical interface for user interaction.

The graphical user interface (GUI) serves as a vital module within the data mining architecture, facilitating communication between users and the data mining system or modules. This module facilitates seamless and effortless interaction between users and the system, alleviating concerns over the intricacies of the process. The graphical user interface (GUI) module collaborates with the data mining system in accordance with the user's task or query, thereby facilitating the presentation of the desired outcomes.

Knowledge Base

This module represents the final component within the data set, wherein it contributes significantly to the comprehensive data mining procedure. This module possesses the capability to assess the stake measure employed for the detection of concealed outcomes and to provide guidance for the search process. The knowledge base module comprises information derived from a user's firsthand encounters, perspectives, and supplementary sources, thereby facilitating the process of data mining. The knowledge base attains inputs and information from the data mining engine in order to acquire dependable and precise information. The knowledge base engages in interaction with the pattern assessment module in order to acquire inputs and subsequently update the stored data within the module.

Integrate Your Meditation Practice With Creative Visualization

In the following chapter, our objective is to integrate the heightened level of concentration achieved from your consistent engagement in meditation and effectively employ it in the technique of imaginative visualization. Develop your meditative practice to such a degree that it imbues the alternate reality you are envisioning with a significant level of vitality.

As previously elucidated in the preceding chapter, it is imperative to undertake this action in order to incite a profound level of emotional engagement within oneself. Rest assured, irrespective of the numerous intellectual deliberations you may engage in or the abundance of information you acquire, the true essence of a belief or experience remains intangible unless it resonates deeply within your core.

Similarly, you possess a distinct and lucid perspective that encompasses a well-constructed and rational trajectory from your current position to the desired pinnacle of achievement. However, the viability of such a plan would be inconsequential as it lacks the necessary emotional authenticity. Visualization fosters the establishment of an emotional element.

Allow me to explain the manner in which it accomplishes this. Initially, you elaborate on the specifics as you engage in the process of visualization. You perform this task within a three-dimensional framework. You're not solely fixated on visual perception. Additionally, you envisage the olfactory, gustatory, tactile, and auditory sensations, as well as the corresponding emotional experience, that would be encountered during the immersion into that alternative realm. It extends beyond mere visual perception. It extends beyond the visual aspects. It is imperative for it to encompass olfactory, auditory, tactile, and gustatory elements. Stated differently, it must be rendered with utmost realism.

Why do this?

What is the underlying rationale for seeking a considerable level of realism in the visualization process? Firstly, you cultivate a heightened sense of urgency. When one engages in visualization without attaining such a heightened level of lucidity, it becomes apparent to the mind that one is merely conjuring an alternate rendition of reality. It's still not real. It remains disconnected from the present reality of your current life.

Ultimately, it's still theoretical. Once your mind apprehends this, employing defensive mechanisms becomes quite effortless.

We all possess an inherent inclination towards comfort. We consistently strive to choose the most effortless course of action. Your cognitive faculties are disinclined to invest the necessary effort to bring about the envisioned outcome; instead, they are prone to disregarding it as a mere hypothetical concept detached from your current actuality.

Alternatively, when one considers three-dimensional visualization and deeply invests in the emotional aspect of their vision, a heightened level of immediacy is cultivated. Your conviction becomes activated, leading you to the understanding that this scenario possesses such vividness that its occurrence becomes plausible. With consistent repetition, the phrase "this can happen" transforms into the certainty that "this will happen."

The secret? Immediacy. The greater the sense of immediacy or impending nature of the feeling, the more probable it becomes that your brain will perceive that vision as an inevitability rather than a mere possibility, particularly when you concentrate on it.

An additional advantage you receive is an increased level of emotional immediacy. It is important to bear in mind that something cannot be considered truly authentic unless it is deeply experienced and felt within one's heart. Without experiencing fear, excitement, a strong sense of purpose, or any semblance of personal drive, even the most meticulously crafted plans will prove ineffectual, as they are solely comprised of factual information and numerical data. They're just logistics. It is imperative that you cultivate a profound and conspicuous sense of urgency, as this heightened awareness would compel you to consistently engage in active pursuits on a daily basis.

Not only do you persist in pondering your vision, but you also articulate it, immerse yourself in the intricate nuances of the emotional thrill it evokes, and take tangible steps towards its fulfillment. This is the point at which your life undergoes a transformation as a result of the alterations in your actions and conduct stemming from your concentrated focus on a specific vision. Thus, I arrive at the ultimate advantage to be gained from 3D visualization, which is emotional commitment.

You begin to perceive your vision as an inherent component of your personal identity. It is now intrinsically connected to you. It is not any longer a creation of your intellect. Rather, it is an inherent aspect of your identity. If one is capable of accomplishing this, it becomes exceedingly difficult to relinquish. You will incessantly chip away at that vision until your mindset undergoes a transformation, consequently influencing your emotional states and tendencies, ultimately resulting in behavioral change.

Solidify the process of meshing through affirmative statements.

Now that you have cultivated your ability to focus with heightened mindfulness on your vision, thereby fostering a profound sense of urgency, emotional intensity, and deep personal commitment, the subsequent undertaking is to solidify this process of integration. To be concise, your objective is to maximize the level of permanency.

What is the process for accomplishing this task? Turn to affirmations. You consistently affirm declarations that manifest your desired vision. Once more, it is difficult to determine a definitive answer as I am unaware of your precise vision. Therefore, it is imperative that you articulate a precise affirmation for your vision.

As an illustration, supposing your aspiration entails residing in a lavish $6 million residence nestled amidst the picturesque Californian hills, you can manifest this vision through the utterance of affirmations that reflect your commitment towards its actualization. For instance, you may express, "I am prepared to materialize this cherished dream through the diligent pursuit of my business plan on a daily basis." "I am fully prepared for the acquisition of this house given my consistent efforts in expanding my professional connections on a daily basis," and so forth.

Your affirmation is required to fulfill the following three criteria. First and foremost, it is imperative that it confirms your preparedness. Furthermore, it is imperative that it validates your eligibility. It is imperative to ensure that you assert your worthiness and deservingness of that vision. It is undesirable to find oneself in a circumstance wherein one experiences feelings of being disingenuous or deceitful. That approach is not deemed feasible. Engaging in such behavior is detrimental to your own success.

Your affirmations should not solely concentrate on your level of preparedness. In essence, it refers to your readiness to proactively pursue your aspirations in the present moment, as well as your deservingness. Indeed, it is imperative that you possess a sense of worthiness toward your vision.

In conclusion, it is imperative to assert your aptitude. You would acquire, if not already possessed, the requisite skills and talents indispensable for fulfilling the work that serves as a catalyst for the realization of your aspirations. It is imperative to understand that your affirmations play a crucial role in building the foundation for effective creative visualization.

Merely engaging in creative visualization falls short. In order to substantiate your claim, it is necessary to provide corroborating evidence, as affirmations have the power to manifest a desired reality.

Your subconscious mind is attentive to the statements you make. As one gradually substitutes negative self-talk with positive affirmations, the subconscious mind becomes attuned to this transformation and actively strives to manifest it in reality. While you may have lacked confidence in the past, consistent affirmation of my confidence will undoubtedly foster a transformation in my demeanor, prompting me to exhibit assuredness and embrace greater levels of risk-taking, ultimately leading to an enhanced sense of confidence. Begin manifesting your desired outcomes by utilizing affirmations. There is no more opportune moment than the present time.

Chapter Three: Techniques for Implementing Visualization

Upon completing the practice of mindfulness meditation, you are prepared to engage in the process of visualizing and deeply engraving vivid mental images depicting your aspirations and desires within the depths of your subconscious. As previously mentioned, employing visualization proves to be a highly efficacious technique for materializing desired outcomes in one's life. The pivotal factor in achieving your objectives and aspirations resides in your unique capacity to envision them. Presented below are the sequential procedures for effectively employing mental imagery to facilitate the manifestation of one's thoughts into tangible actualities.

Create a vivid mental imagery

After completing the practice of meditation and achieving a state of heightened concentration and tranquility, you may proceed to contemplate your aspirations and ambitions in life. Please ensure that the picture is crisp and vivid. The subconscious mind comprehends distinct visual representations. Enhancing lucidity will expedite the manifestation of your desires by your subconscious mind.

Ensure that you are conceptualizing with thorough attention to detail. For instance, should you aspire to embark on a future holiday in the picturesque Santorini, Greece, endeavor to envision yourself in that very destination, allowing your imagination to transport you there. It is essential to meticulously visualize and incorporate every intricate aspect in your mental reconstruction. Imagine your hotel room. Consider the sensation of strolling through the cobblestone passageways of Santorini. What is the olfactory experience associated with the sea? Could you provide me with a description of the appearance of the sky? Have you encountered captivating individuals from the local community? Did you swim or did you try sunbathing? Did you venture to that place unaccompanied or were you joined by someone?

If your intention is to start a family, envision yourself entering matrimony with your envisioned perfect partner. Envision yourself or your partner conceiving a child. What is your desired number of offspring? What is your desired number of daughters? What is your desired number of offspring in terms of sons? Could you please provide a description of their appearance? Do they exhibit qualities of kindness, affection, intelligence, and playfulness? Exercise attention to detail when engaging in visualization.

Involve Your Other Senses

In order for creative visualization to yield desired outcomes, it is imperative to engage all of your other senses. It is essential that you employ your olfactory, gustatory, auditory, and tactile senses. To effectively materialize something uncomplicated such as a cup of coffee, it is imperative to visualize oneself in physical contact with said cup. One must envision oneself partaking in the act of sipping. Contemplate the flavor sensations that would be experienced in such a scenario. Imagine the aroma. Envision the warmth emitted by the coffee as it makes contact with your taste buds.

To acquire a mental image of succeeding in an examination, envision yourself actively engaged in the examination process. What do you see? What do you hear? Envision yourself documenting the accurate responses. Envision yourself presenting the paper to your professor and subsequently, envision receiving the examination paper returned with the sought-after outcome.

Be In the Moment

The primary distinction between visualization and daydreaming resides in the necessity of experiencing and envisioning the desired outcome as if it has already been accomplished.

In order to attain a new, lucrative occupation, it is imperative to cultivate a mindset of perceiving oneself as already possessing said job. It is imperative to envision yourself already presiding at your new workstation and becoming acquainted with your new colleagues. One must envision the aromas that permeate the new work environment and take into consideration the tactile sensation of the carpet under one's feet. Envision yourself adorned in immaculate corporate attire, seamlessly executing our daily responsibilities. It is essential to develop a sense of it. It is imperative that you cultivate the perception that the desired outcome is already being realized.

In order to acquire a new residence, it is essential to cultivate a sense of already inhabiting it. Envision the hues exhibited by the walls, the arrangement of the sofas, and the luxurious expanse of the king-sized bed. Envision the presence of the pool, the garden, and the scenic vista. Envision the sensations evoked by the act of descending onto the medieval-inspired couch, as well as the refreshing immersion into the confines of your pool.

It is crucial to genuinely experience and envision oneself already living the life of one's dreams.

Have fun

Enjoy the feeling. Have fun. One should not perceive visualization as a burdensome task. One should endeavor to remain calm and composed without succumbing to any feelings of pressure or tension while undertaking this task. It is of great significance to experience a sense of levity and elation. Elicit the sensation of joy that will inevitably accompany the realization of your aspirations and ambitions. Unleash the full spectrum of positive energies that permeate the cosmos.

Please refrain from envisioning any obstacles or challenges.

It is of utmost significance to refrain from envisioning any form of obstruction or challenge during the process of visualization. Everything should be flawless. In the event that you detect any mental barriers arising, promptly dismiss them and substitute them with constructive thoughts.

Pablo Picasso, the renowned artist, once famously stated that all that you can envision within your mind is brought to life in reality. There are boundless possibilities awaiting in terms of what one can undertake to achieve. One can attain unlimited possibilities. The possibilities are limitless. One can assume any desired identity and attain the desired level of success simply by instilling detailed, optimistic imagery into one's subconscious. Over time, you will be astonished by the advantageous transformations that will occur in your life.

An additional step within the framework of the innovative visualization treatment pertains to the imperative task of cultivating a sense of trust in the notion that one's desired outcome has already been manifested in the present moment. This does not pertain to harboring wishful thoughts or exhibiting self-betrayal. It pertains to the recognition of the underlying veracity of truth generation and demonstrating a form of assurance that substantiates intangible assertions.

Your thought process

To engage in cogitation: To perceive an idea involves attaining its utmost comprehension. There is no longer a necessity to contemplate it. If you are confident that you have a clear intention in your current situation, there is no need to linger in a state of anticipation or uncertainty regarding its whereabouts, as you possess it in the present moment. During the course of your visualization sessions, rest assured that you possess the capacity to fully immerse yourself in the positive experience associated with the desired outcome. The teachings of Jesus immaculately capture the essence of proper thought: "Whatever things you ask for in prayer, believe that you receive them, and you will have them" (Mark 11:24).

Could you please elaborate on the precise methodology for adopting the appropriate mindset, and strategizing one's thoughts?

Relax utilizing the recreational techniques outlined hereafter.

Please locate a quiet environment where you can ensure minimal interruptions for at least 30 minutes. Assume a seated position in a well-appointed chair, ensuring your feet are placed firmly on the floor, your back is properly supported, and your hands are relaxed in your lap. If you so choose, you may opt to engage in relaxation, provided that you can refrain from succumbing to sleep during the course of the procedure.

Close your eyes and perform three to five deep diaphragmatic breaths. Inhale deeply and gradually through your nose, allowing your abdomen to slightly expand or protrude. This facilitates diaphragmatic relaxation and enhances the influx of additional air into the lungs.

Please temporarily refrain from inhaling and exhale slowly through your mouth, allowing your abdominal area to return to its normal state.

In order to ensure the proper utilization of appropriate breathing techniques, it is recommended to place your hand on your abdominal area while engaging in the process of respiration. This is the correct method for inhaling air. Practice independently to effortlessly inhale in this manner during your sessions of mental imagery.

Systematically diminish your emotional state from twenty-five to one, all the while remembering to inhale deeply. If it is found that counting in reverse fails to induce a state of relaxation, one may wish to consider commencing from fifty or a higher numerical value as deemed necessary. In like manner, when employing the appropriate methodology, you may discover that commencing the enumeration from as modest a digit as 10 is sufficient to attain the identical state of tranquility.

Furthermore, provide your mind unequivocal reassurance by acknowledging the possessions you currently possess, such as the secure shelter you inhabit, the splendid view you enjoy, the dependable vehicle at your disposal, or simply the knowledge and certainty of your forthcoming income. Please bear in mind the precise manner in which your cognitive faculties and physical state react to the presence of such a definite certainty. One is highly probable to experience a complete absence of stress, worry, surprise, desire, but rather only the sense of peace and calmness that stems from awareness. Immerse yourself in the profound understanding of what it truly means to possess something. Consistently engage in this exercise and before long, you shall acquire the skill of conceptualization, permitting you to effortlessly recreate and evoke the very essence of the desired experiences you seek to encounter during your visualization sessions.

What Factors Are Impeding Your Progress Or Inhibiting Your Success?

Prior to delving into the strategies for manifestation, it is crucial to examine and unearth any obstacles impeding your progress.

In the forthcoming chapter, we shall explore the rationales that impede individuals from attaining their aspirations. This encompasses attitudes towards finances, emotions of inadequacy, perceptions of oneself or others, and, finally, reasons behind the ineffectiveness of affirmations.

To attain prosperity, affection, and ample opportunities, it is essential to wholeheartedly concentrate on these ideals. The cosmos will align with your thoughts and emotions.

Should you direct your attention towards fear, scarcity, and pessimism, the Cosmos will not solely reciprocate these sentiments, but will magnify and reflect them back to you.

As previously mentioned, metaphysical laws exhibit impartiality. They do not bestow rewards nor inflict punishments. They will merely react to that which receives our focus.

There exists a classic song that articulates the concept of wealth accumulation for the affluent and an increased family size for the less fortunate. The wealthy amass their fortune through their concerted attention to financial accumulation and indulging in the luxuries that monetary affluence provides. The underprivileged individuals express concern regarding the payment of bills, sustenance, provision of groceries and healthcare, as well as their inability to concentrate due to their limited resources. Each group is benefiting from their respective experiences.

The outcomes you receive from the Universe are a direct reflection of your thoughts and beliefs. Hence, it is of utmost importance to diligently monitor your thoughts, desires, and expressions. Declaring, even in a playful manner, that you lack the financial means to purchase that new handbag will yield the corresponding outcome.

Inclusive of the Laws of Attraction, Correspondence, and the Law of Cause and Effect, I am inclined to incorporate the Law of Circulation. The principle of circulation necessitates an uninterrupted state of movement. If you impede the flow at any point in the cycle, you obstruct the influx of positive experiences in your life. If one experiences a sense of inadequacy or lack of worthiness, it impedes the smooth flow of financial circulation.

If one experiences discomfort when receiving a gift or even a compliment, the underlying issue does not primarily pertain to financial matters, but rather stems from a sense of personal inadequacy.

Beliefs about Money

The concept of money is morally neutral, possessing neither inherent goodness nor wickedness. It is purely the commodity we presently employ to procure commodities and services. In ages past, we engaged in the exchange of beads and seashells.

A significant number of individuals experience a complex emotional dynamic regarding money, characterized by a blend of affection and trepidation.

From my perspective, the apprehension towards money originated during my childhood. During my Sunday School class, I was informed that money served as the root of all malevolence, and if I harbored an affection for monetary possessions, I would ultimately face damnation. Oh my goodness, I did not desire to be consigned to damnation. I desired to attain a state of celestial bliss. Additionally, I was gripped by trepidation due to the presence of imaginary creatures beneath my sleeping quarters and unsettling sounds emanating from beyond my window.

As I matured, I came to the realization that the existence of monsters was merely fictitious. The boogeyman did not exist and the noise originating from outside my window was simply an overgrown tree branch that required pruning.

Nevertheless, the notion that money bore malevolence persisted within the depths of my subconscious psyche. The frequently expressed assertions derived from my parents that I was undeserving. Over the course of time, the integration of my perspectives regarding money and the experience of inadequacy became deeply ingrained within my psyche, impeding my journey towards achieving financial prosperity over an extensive period.

It required a significant duration for me to comprehend that I was a cherished offspring of the divine, deserving of every favorable aspect in life. To eliminate those thoughts and feelings, a substantial amount of books, tapes, and

CDs were utilized, alongside extensive introspective contemplation.

What are your opinions and convictions regarding wealth and finances? Do you experience discomfort in accepting financial compensation? How does one experience a sense of unease in the abdomen or feelings of remorse when indulging in personal desires with minimal expenditure? Do you experience any reservations or uncertainties in accepting financial compensation or in seeking a salary increase?

To gain insight into the nature of your financial connection, acquire a one-dollar note and grasp it within your palm. Please, kindly close your eyes and engage in deep introspection, allowing yourself to delve into your thoughts and emotions regarding the concept of money. Allow the funds to communicate with you and attentively heed your inner monologue.

Envision yourself as the recipient of funds and subsequently imagine yourself transferring the funds to another individual. Are you experiencing a sensation of tightness in your throat or a feeling of tension in your abdomen? Do you experience any muscular constriction in your body? Do you experience a momentary pause in your heartbeat, or do you sense a discernible retreat of energy in your sacral chakra?

In ancient times, during our habitation of caves, we paid heed to the cues of our own physical beings. We remained vigilant and innately cognizant of the impending peril. In light of this, our very existence hinged upon our faculties of perception. At that juncture, we were acutely cognizant of the fluctuations in air pressure and promptly sought refuge upon detecting alterations in the atmospheric conditions. In the past, we displayed vigilance towards unfamiliar individuals and closely observed their nonverbal cues as indicators of their intentions, determining whether they were amicable or posed a threat. We attentively heeded our intuition and placed our trust in it.

In contemporary society, it has become commonplace to overlook the importance of attentively heeding the messages conveyed by our bodies. We disregard such cautions and concern ourselves with adhering to political correctness. Your physique will derive great pleasure from your attentive receptiveness, and it will gladly furnish you with the responses you are in pursuit of.

What insights does your physique provide regarding financial matters?

I would like you to mentally envision yourself occupying a seat at your kitchen table, engaged in the act of attending to a financial obligation. Do you diligently pen your check with an abundance of joy and gratitude to express appreciation for the satisfactory service rendered? Alternatively, do you apprehensively observe the gradual decrease in your monetary funds? Please observe and take note of all physical and emotional sensations encountered as you allocate your financial resources. Your physical being serves as an indicator of your innate intuition.

Your bodily responses serve as evidential markers of your fundamental beliefs. Occasionally, merely recognizing detrimental thoughts or emotions can facilitate their eradication.

In order to overcome any financial obstacles in your life, engage in the act of giving. Develop the habit of donating money without experiencing any discomfort or hesitation. Engage in the exercise of accepting a compliment graciously without exceeding a simple expression of gratitude. In the event of encountering any limitations, ascertain and remove them until only appreciation remains. Continuously engage in the activity until you sense the euphoria of the encounter and acquire a profound sense of assurance that the funds you have generously bestowed will ultimately come back to you.

As you settle the payment for your meal, envision the monetary exchange emanating from you towards the server, the proprietor of the establishment, and the diligent farmer who invests in procuring the seeds. Experience the joy derived from each exchange facilitated by every individual in the economic network. Observe as your funds are transferred to financial institutions, enterprises, and individuals who derive the positive effects that you have set in motion. Experience the joy that the employees derive from being able to fulfill their housing obligations or provide their children with necessary toys and nourishment.

Funds willingly and benevolently bestowed will come back to you, magnified. Develop the ability to express appreciation when giving and receiving monetary resources.

Release any pessimistic notions you may harbor regarding finances. Swap out those thoughts with a mindset of appreciation by graciously and enthusiastically receiving the funds, funds that you are deserving of accepting and encountering.

Engage in the practice of cultivating the art of accepting with grace. Maintain a mindset of receptiveness towards financial resources and acquire the skill of expressing gratitude. Expressing anything other than gratitude would be regarded as a disservice to the generosity of the provider. Express gratitude to the benefactor, express gratitude to a higher power, and invoke a divine blessing upon the financial resources.

I have observed that individuals who struggle with accepting monetary compensation also encounter challenges when it comes to accepting compliments. If one experiences unease upon receiving a compliment, one should refrain from immediately responding with a dismissive remark about the age of one's attire or disregarding the compliment. By disregarding a kind word or thought, one demonstrates a lack of respect for the individual's opinion, while simultaneously conveying to the broader cosmic order that they do not consider themselves deserving of such benevolent expressions. Engage in the act of diligently rehearsing expressions of gratitude until you acquire the ability to receive a compliment with poise.

It is essential to maintain a continuous circulation of funds. It is acceptable to contribute to your savings or retain it for a prosperous future; however, abstaining from spending it due to apprehension about its return is unnecessary.

Reside within the principles of the Laws of Attraction and Circulation, and a perpetual stream of wealth, affection, and prosperity will manifest in your existence.

Please repeat after me, "I hereby embrace love, good health, harmony, and prosperity as integral aspects of my existence." I derive great pleasure from the continuous influx of economic prosperity in my personal circumstances. I contribute significantly and exhibit financial responsibility by ensuring that my bills are promptly settled, aware of the continuous influx of money into my life. I am deserving of all that is good. I am deserving of a continuous flow of financial prosperity. Thus, it is."

Another commonly held belief that inhibits individuals is the concept of ego, although its connotation may differ from what is commonly understood.

Ego

The term Ego originates from the Latin personal pronoun I. The Ego can be defined as the mental construct that represents our self-perception. It constitutes the collective assemblage of our self-perception, which occasionally becomes intertwined with the external impressions and evaluations made by others.

In the realm of vocabulary, the terms ego or egotistical tend to be associated with an unfavorable connotation, as they are typically employed to depict individuals who display characteristics of vanity, boastfulness, self-absorption, and strong-willed opinions. We hold the belief that the attribution of egotism is unseemly when applied to others, and particularly when self-applied.

There exists an alternative aspect of the self, as insufficient ego or lack thereof can yield equal levels of harm and incapacitation. This facet of the ego communicates to the individual, "I lack worthiness." "I am not worthy of goodness, affection, or achievement." Should the ego genuinely hold these beliefs, I can assure you that a dismal existence and unfavorable results lie ahead.

For numerous individuals, negative self-perceptions were instilled during their early years when they were subjected to disparaging remarks from parents, educators, or peers, or may have originated within the recesses of our introspective inner dialogue.

The sentiments of inadequacy are as ingrained within us as the verses of a nostalgic tune that persistently linger in the recesses of our thoughts. If left unaddressed, these enduring harmonies infiltrate every facet of our existence. Experiencing a sense of inadequacy can impede our progress towards achieving success. It will prevent us from attaining boundless opulence, happiness, excellent well-being, and even affection.

Verbal remarks can only inflict harm if one chooses to accept their validity. You shall not attain success until you comprehend your inherent worthiness of every favorable outcome.

The belief that success should be attainable for everyone, but clinging to this notion may confine oneself within a profound state of dissatisfaction. You are presented with the option to either persist in this abyss of erroneous narratives or elevate yourself from a skewed perspective of your genuine self.

You possess extraordinary qualities, embodying perfection, entirety, and fulfillment. Please re-read the sentence with careful consideration, allowing sufficient time for each word to be fully comprehended. While doing so, take a moment to internalize and deeply connect with each word, allowing their significance to resonate within every fiber of your being, as this sentence encapsulates your true essence. You are special. You possess inherent perfection in your current state. You possess inherent wholeness and completeness.

It is imperative for individuals to cultivate a well-rounded, autonomous, and unaffected self-perception, detached from external influences.

At present, it would be opportune to document your reflections and sentiments regarding the concept of achievement.

According to a sales principle, there are two underlying motivations behind any action: the actual reason and the one that appears favorable.

Your unfounded, ego-driven trepidation may lead you to believe that escaping your unfulfilling employment or embracing a lifestyle revered by others is an unattainable feat. In the present scenario, you justify that you possess the qualities of a competent parent, partner, and citizen by opting to remain in the position, as it aligns with your sense of duty and responsibility. Does your response represent the true rationale or is it merely an attempt to create an appealing impression? If the underlying cause for such sentiments lies in a sense of inadequacy, as though expressing a belief that you are undeserving of anything greater than an unfulfilling occupation, I implore you to dismiss such notions of unworthiness and instead seek opportunities to manifest your aspirations.

Upon recognizing and revealing the underlying cause for maintaining employment in an unsatisfactory position, one will progress and advance in their life endeavors.

The notion that one is undeserving holds no truth. In order to overcome sentiments of inadequacy, it is necessary to elevate your sense of self-worth.

Affirmations are highly beneficial; nevertheless, it is imperative to hold an unwavering belief in the authenticity of your affirmations.

To alter your self-perception, commence by compiling a catalogue of favorable qualities pertaining to your character. This serves as your initial point of reference.

Take the time to record and acknowledge the positive attributes that you possess, those which are marked by goodness, strength, and benevolence. Upon embarking on this personal reflection, I could merely perceive a solitary positive aspect of my being. It was only after several days and weeks had elapsed that I was able to augment my roster, yet during this time, I discerned the commendable attributes inherent within myself. Contrary to initial perceptions, I did not possess an unattractive, vulnerable quality similar to that of a duckling. Over time, I discovered a swan gazing back at me in the reflection of the mirror. The positive characteristics were inherently present; due to my self-doubt and lack of self-esteem, it took me considerable time to recognize them.

Continue diligently to compile your catalog, diligently filling each successive page as you develop a comprehensive awareness and comprehension of your authentic self. Please regularly examine your roster and make daily additions to it. This objective remains incumbent upon you until such time as you attain a thorough comprehension of your true identity. Alongside the expansion of your list, the augmentation of your self-esteem, sense of pride, and appreciation of your inherent beauty will also develop.

Cultivate self-love and gratitude on a daily basis, ensuring that you dedicate yourself to performing at least one act of kindness or self-care each day. Empower yourself to become the focal point of your own life!

Do things you love. Engaging in activities that bring you joy is a testament to your self-worth and the inherent beauty within your being. Taking action serves as confirmation of your internal narrative regarding your inherent worth. As you engage in actions that cultivate self-care through the genuine act of self-love, you will gradually develop a conviction and gain a profound understanding of your authentic self. These minor aspects gradually develop into a sense of personal value.

Schedule a personal appointment with yourself to partake in a leisurely stroll, engage in literary pursuits, or engage in any activity that brings about a sense of elevation to your being. Please undertake any actions that will enhance your sense of importance, as you truly deserve it.

You have long been aware of your unique qualities, and now is the opportune moment to genuinely embrace and revel in your extraordinary essence.

Affirm my worth ceaselessly on a perpetual basis, until you ascertain its veracity. I can provide you with complete assurance that you will discover an elevated manifestation of your own persona, one that is deserving of every facet of triumph.

Reside within an environment devoid of prejudgment. Cease harboring judgments towards others, as your propensity to criticize shall inevitably beget retribution upon yourself. The presence of judgment and the unwillingness to forgive oneself for past mistakes, combined with negative self-dialogue, restrict one's ability to move forward and impede the natural flow of life. Reside within a zone void of criticism or prejudice. The constraints in which you confine yourself will be relinquished. Residing within a zone devoid of scrutiny will engender a sense of liberation, thereby allowing one to experience a heightened sense of buoyancy.

Furthermore, when considering past disappointments, please remember that you consistently demonstrated your utmost efforts and made the most favorable decisions. In a similar vein, I urge you to extend your forgiveness, just as you would graciously pardon a close companion, and release any lingering resentments stemming from previous actions that burden your spirit. They do not constitute a component of your present experience. Indeed, as a result of those occurrences, you have blossomed into the exquisite individual you are today.

Gain a comprehensive understanding that your purpose in life is not to adopt a victim mentality but to embrace the role of a protagonist.

Direct your attention towards actions and elements that bring you a sense of satisfaction and contribute to enriching your personal experience. You can only attain financial abundance when you internalize and genuinely embrace it.

By enhancing your personal identity, you will encounter favorable transformations in your environment. Elevate your thoughts, emotions, and vibrational energy; thereby, you will manifest a fresh existence characterized by a proficient and harmonious sense of self.

Allocate a portion of your time to meticulously documenting the benevolent actions you undertake and the extent to which you have positively impacted the lives of others. Please document your achievements, positive statements, and the aspirations you have successfully realized. Perceive yourself in the same light that I do. An individual who possesses the merit and is deserving of achievement.

It is your inherently destined path to partake in the fullness of life, and to thrive in the presence of abundant blessings.

In the context of your contemplation and mental imagery, envision yourself attaining your objective. Have faith in the attainability of your dream. The current moment represents the realization of the past.

The Almighty would never bestow upon you a vision devoid of actualization. It is in the divine's desire for your achievement and prosperity to be realized.

What Strategies Can Be Employed To Effectively Harness The Power Of Visualization In Order To Achieve Desired Outcomes?

To effectively utilize the power of visualization, it is imperative that one enhances their level of focus and concentration. To cultivate strong interpersonal bonds, it is imperative to alleviate feelings of stress and tension. Make an effort to center your attention and alleviate any stray thoughts from your consciousness. An unsettled mentality will hinder one's chances of achieving success in life, thereby amplifying feelings of discontentment and disillusionment. The incorporation of the Focus into your daily routine has the potential to enhance your overall sense of enjoyment and satisfaction in life. Maintaining a mindset that is centered and devoid of distractions is paramount to attaining both fulfillment and achievements in one's life.

Develop a strong determination

To effectively alleviate distractions and extraneous thoughts, it is imperative to foster a resolute determination to allocate your time solely towards substantial tasks. Commit to yourself that you will utilize your time effectively and not squander it. The individuals allocate the majority of their time contemplating the notion of postponing their tasks. Develop a consistent practice of promptly completing tasks rather than procrastinating and deferring them to a later date.

Eliminate the tendency to procrastinate.

Procrastination is deemed an unfavorable habit, given its tendency to prioritize trivial tasks over the completion of essential ones. It would be beneficial for you to acquire an understanding of the significance associated with each task and subsequently organize your daily schedule accordingly. Acquire the skill of assigning precedence to crucial operations.

Establish Your Daily Objective

It is important to regularly establish and review your goals as this will aid in sustaining your focus and directing your attention solely towards routine tasks. The objective is accompanied by a predetermined timeframe, and in order to achieve any objective within the specified period, it is imperative that you devote your complete focus and dedication to it. Compose your objectives, and upon the achievement of said objectives, you may consider granting yourself a reward as an incentive to enhance your motivation.

Sustain Your Physical Fitness

Enhance your self-discipline in order to cultivate a cognitive state of concentration, as the absence of control will hinder your ability to evade diversions. For instance, while the allure of indulging in a film may be enticing, it is imperative that you exercise restraint in order to refrain from watching one until you have fulfilled your obligations. Please exercise self-discipline when undertaking important tasks. It will enhance your efficiency and elevate your rate of achievement.

Increase Your Wisdom

Expand your understanding and endeavor to become an immovable force in order to eliminate all inhibiting factors. It is advised to strive for a harmonious equilibrium between one's personal and professional spheres, as matters of the heart, aspirations, and career hold significant significance in one's overall life. Maintain equilibrium between both internal and external circumstances to exert influence over one's life. Enhance your intellectual capacity in order to achieve equilibrium between pragmatic and individual responsibilities.

Minimize the Utilization of Internet

The internet plays a pivotal role in both educational and personal domains, although it harbors numerous distractions that detrimentally impact one's productivity. If it is genuinely imperative for you to utilize the internet, please bear in mind that you possess ample crucial responsibilities to attend to. Following the completion of your tasks, you have the opportunity to engage in recreational activities such as gaming, music listening, and film enjoyment.

Reduce the Consumption of Coffee and Chocolate

The desire for coffee and chocolate has the potential to induce anxiety, thus it is advisable to refrain from excessive consumption of these items. It is recommended to partake in the consumption of green tea, milk, and other nutritious beverages to enhance your focus and reap numerous health advantages. It is anticipated that by engaging in this activity, your stress levels will be diminished and your ability to focus and concentrate will be enhanced.

Affix a Signage to Your Door

In the event that you are engaged in a task of significance, consider the merits of closing your door and displaying a sign that states "Occupied." This measure would effectively discourage the attention of others, as it would serve as a clear indication that you are currently inaccessible. You may record your designated working hours to inform others of your availability.

Increase Your Motivation

Motivation plays a pivotal role in one's life as it is imperative for undertaking arduous and sustained endeavors. It grants you the ability to promptly fulfill your assignments. Maintain your attention on the advantages of the objectives in order to enhance your motivation to complete the task. Make an effort to adhere to deadlines in order to enhance your level of accomplishment, as consistent success will grant you the opportunity to allocate your attention to additional responsibilities. It will facilitate the creation of a purposeful existence for you.

Positive Expectancy Meditation

To be directed towards the narrator: This particular piece is intended to be appreciated as a deliberate and measured contemplation. Each sentence should be enunciated unhurriedly, and a pause of approximately twenty seconds is advised before proceeding to the next sentence, unless indicated otherwise.

Welcome to this facilitated exercise specifically crafted to aid you in visualizing and manifesting your perception of an ideal and fulfilling life. I kindly request that you assume a relaxed and comfortable posture on the floor, within a tranquil and serene environment.

Please ensure that you are in a quiet environment and that all electronic devices are switched off to avoid any disruptions.

Now, please kindly proceed to gently close your eyes and proceed to take three deep breaths.

Make an effort to clear your mind by recognizing and then releasing each fleeting thought.

Once your mind attains a state of tranquility and vacancy, redirect your undivided attention towards your physical self.

Position your hands upon your chest, allowing the untamed energy dwelling within to flow unrestricted.

After undergoing the physical activity that took place yesterday, one can reasonably expect a seamless and unhindered circulation of vitality throughout their physique, purged of any obstructive elements such as negative energies and lingering memories of prior occurrences.

Envision and sense the pervasive nature of this energy as it permeates every corner, emanating from your head and feet, enveloping you in its radiant luminescence and boundless affection.

Observe as the entire space is engulfed in the radiance emanating from this luminosity, forming a protective and empowering aura of optimistic, untapped energy. It is within this ambiance that we shall harness our creative visualization abilities to envision a prosperous and promising future in store for you.

At this moment, I kindly request that you harness all of your affirmative energy to focus your attention on your respiration.

Make an attempt to take in breath gradually, ensuring each inhalation spans a duration of seven counts, subsequently pausing for seven counts, and finally exhaling slowly for another seven counts, with an additional pause of seven counts to complete the process.

Take a deep breath, counting to seven as you do so. Retain your breath, counting to seven. Release your breath gradually, counting to seven once more, and then hold it again for a count of seven. Perform this action a total of seven instances, at a measured pace. (Repeat seven times.)

You may now resume your regular breathing rhythm and position both of your hands upon your heart.

Experience the palpable force emanating from it, encompassing your being, and serving as a shield for your safety.

Delve into the depths of your being, where the core of that energy resides.

Dispense with any apprehension or concern; you hold the reins within this domain... This area holds profound significance to you.

Presently, I request that you harness and channel the collective positivity that has been cultivated throughout our shared voyage, and employ it to construct a vivid vision of your forthcoming prospects.

What kind of life do you desire? What factors would contribute to your overall happiness and contentment?

Do not engage in censorship or critical evaluation of your thoughts; instead, wholeheartedly embrace them with love and acceptance.

Now, envision a hypothetical scenario wherein you are requested to articulate a meticulously constructed ideal day, six months from the present moment.

Contemplate an extraordinary occasion so remarkable that it can be relived countless times, consistently evoking feelings of sheer bliss.

Irrespective of whether your aspirations pertain to employment, affection, wellness, or any other domain, it is crucial to acknowledge that this journey is uniquely yours, as is your personal vision.

Regardless of your interpretation of happiness and contentment, now is the opportune time for you to forge a constructive path towards your future.

Exude self-assurance and assertiveness in your visualizations, harnessing the immense positive energy that you have unleashed through your diligent preparation in preceding days.

Strive for utmost precision, endeavor to envision every intricate detail in your imagination.

Imagine waking up in the morning during your perfect day. What is your emotional state? Are you currently situated in your private residence or in a location of remarkable uniqueness? Are you accompanied by anyone or are you solitary?

Experience the sensation of the gravitational force exerted on your body as it rests upon the mattress, perceive the subtle rustling of the bed sheets, immerse yourself in the olfactory cues and auditory elements that compose an idyllic morning.

Take pleasure in crafting the ideal environment, a sanctuary where you can experience security and tranquility.

Now envision yourself embarking upon your day and departing from your abode: which destination do you intend to visit and what activities do you plan to engage in upon arrival?

Envision all the locations through which you traverse, irrespective of their familiarity or unfamiliarity to you.

Immerse yourself in the full spectrum of their colors, captivating scents, and resonating sounds. Observe the celestial expanse: is it adorned with sunlight or veiled in cascading raindrops during your idyllic day? Are the raindrops delicately descending upon your skin or is the breeze tenderly brushing against your face?

Engage all your senses: feel, observe, and perceive every detail around you. You are an integral part of this location and time, and they are interconnected with your being.

You have reached your destination at this time. Observe your surroundings; what is the sensation of arriving at this place at last?

Which sentiments are currently pervading your being: are they feelings of delight, elation, or contentment? Are you currently experiencing this moment in companionship or solitude?

Envision the profound sensations that will arise upon the actualization of all your long-awaited aspirations.

Do not impose constraints upon yourself: seize this opportune day, seize this auspicious moment, and engage in whatever activity you desire, be it reclining upon your sleeping quarters or partaking in a exhilarating bungee jumping adventure amidst the wilderness.

We are presently engaged in constructing the very foundations of your joy, contentment, and prospects.

Please inhale deeply three times and grant yourself a brief moment to thoroughly savor and appreciate this experience. (Pause for 30 seconds.)

Now, I kindly request that you transition the imagery from your mind to your heart.

Presented herein lies the wellspring of your emotional prowess and the nexus of the positive energy meticulously cultivated in preceding days.

Kindly employ the designated confidential term at present, repetitively reiterating it within your thoughts on three occasions, whilst directing all encompassing spiritual vigor towards the mental visualization.

Enhance it with the intensified brightness, heightened boldness, and expanded size that can be achieved through the strength of your emotions.

Do not hinder your progress, set lofty goals and employ all of your available resources to manifest that vision within yourself.

Direct all your affection and appreciation towards the future, allowing yourself to embrace the belief in the reality you are actively shaping.

Harness the potential of your heart and channel the abundance of inner energy to manifest that vision into actuality, promptly.

Allow yourself to embrace a profound sense of optimism regarding the prospects of your future, permitting these positive sentiments to permeate your being, infiltrating every fiber of your physical form, until a harmonious union is established with them.

Observe as the envisioned manifestation of an ideal day commences its onset, propelling your reality into motion at this precise moment.

Envisage, if you will, the emotions that shall inevitably arise within you upon the arrival of this auspicious day: the profound delight, the utmost fulfillment, the deep affection, and every other sentiment that is destined to overwhelm your being.

Envision yourself embodying the individual you have perpetually aspired to become, experiencing the existence you have perpetually longed for.

Now, take a brief pause to unwind and duly recognize the nature of your recent encounter. Please allow me a moment of pause.

Shift your attention back to your breathing, with a deliberate focus on the expansion and contraction of your abdomen as you inhale and exhale.

Inhale and slowly exhale. Reiterate the sentence periodically over the course of one minute.

Reclaim your bodily consciousness by first directing your attention to your feet, followed by your legs, back, abdomen, arms, hands, facial region, and ultimately, your head.

Sensate the sensation of your physical form resting upon the earth, with hands gently placed upon your chest, while surroundings reverberate with auditory stimuli.

Gently redirect your attention to the present moment, allowing yourself to gradually reconnect with your surroundings.

Inhale deeply three times, and once you feel prepared, proceed to unveil your eyes.

Please pause briefly, then rise and perform a full body stretch after a few seconds.

Reestablish your connection with the ground by rhythmically pressing your feet onto the floor, thereby replenishing yourself with self-compassion.

Congratulations, you have successfully concluded the fourth stage of this endeavor!

Attracting Money With Visualization

Visualization can serve a multitude of objectives; however, one particularly advantageous application involves cultivating a sense of prosperity within oneself and magnetizing an increased flow of financial resources. One may question the potential benefits of visualizing simplistic imagery within one's mind in order to manifest desired outcomes. However, upon deeper contemplation, it becomes evident that maintaining a steadfast focus on scarcity inevitably leads to a mindset that anticipates unfavorable circumstances and consequently influences one's thoughts and actions in a manner that accentuates deficiency. Essentially, this perpetuates a cycle wherein one continues to experience a dearth of abundance in their life.

Conversely, when one shifts their perspective from perceiving scarcity to cultivating a more pervasive sense of abundance, they will notice a change in their cognitive processes and subsequent behavior that can lead to increased prosperity. Not only will you gain a deeper sense of gratitude for the abundance in your current life, but you will also cultivate a more favorable mental state that enables you to readily identify and seize upon exceptional opportunities as they arise.

To achieve optimal outcomes, it is advisable to incorporate visualization as a habitual practice, as altering one's mental perspective necessitates consistent reinforcement. You have the option to engage in your visualization exercises either in the early morning, immediately prior to retiring for the evening, or at any juncture throughout the day when you have a brief window of time available.

What categories of objects should you mentally depict? To begin with, envision yourself possessing an abundance of financial resources. Envision a scenario where you possess the capability to effortlessly settle your financial obligations and have an abundance of disposable income for recreational pursuits, philanthropy, and prudent saving towards a more promising tomorrow. Ensure that you create these visualizations with meticulous attention to detail, including aspects such as the attire you are wearing, the residence in which you reside, the vehicle you operate, and your demeanor during your daily undertakings.

The inclusion of meticulous details holds significance due to their ability to evoke deep emotions, thereby engrossing individuals in a vivid firsthand experience. This immersive encounter enables the subconscious mind to readily embrace these visions. Consider, for a moment, the profound sentiment that would accompany the possession of abundant financial resources. What kind of mindset would you adopt if financial concerns were no longer a factor for you? Incorporate these thoughts and emotions into your visualization exercises, ensuring their intensity and authenticity.

Subsequently, it is crucial to ensure that you are not negating all the significant effort exerted during your visualization exercises by harboring thoughts and engaging in behaviors that contradict the manifestation of your desired outcomes into your existence.

Refrain from dedicating time to fretting over a lack of financial resources, experiencing distress regarding monetary obligations, or succumbing to anxiousness concerning one's income. As soon as you initiate these actions, you promptly redirect your attention towards a mindset characterized by deficiency, thus perpetuating the robust cycle of scarcity.

It is imperative to ensure that you do not restrict the potential avenues through which income can manifest in your life. A cautious approach would entail refraining from placing excessive emphasis solely on the prospect of winning the lottery, as this course of action would impede the exploration of alternate opportunities. Please bear in mind that financial resources have the potential to manifest in a multitude of ways, many of which may be unforeseen. It is crucial to maintain an open mindset, embracing all possible opportunities, and allowing your optimistic perspective to draw in larger and more remarkable accomplishments beyond your current realm of imagination.

Techniques in Monetary Visualization

The application of money visualization techniques facilitates the attraction of increased financial resources and prosperity into one's life. Don't worry though. The methods of attracting wealth that I am about to share are straightforward and enjoyable to engage in.

There is no cause for fear or embarrassment. We all aspire to increase our monetary resources as it affords us the opportunity to elevate our standard of living. If you are prepared for some exceptional recommendations to enhance the inflow of financial resources into your life, proceed with reading!

Technique 1 for Visualizing Wealth: Eliminating the Feelings of Shame.

The initial step that should be taken is to eliminate any negative emotions that are present. Experiencing feelings of discomfiture when picturing oneself as affluent and satisfied will only guarantee its ultimate lack of success.

If one desires to effectively achieve their goals and acquire abundant wealth, it is essential to acknowledge that there is no inherent flaw in the practice of visualization. If it proves advantageous, consider the extent to which one can provide assistance to others when possessing increased financial means.

Financial Visualization Technique #2: Establishing a Visual Representation Board.

Crafting a vision board proves to be an engaging method for attracting prosperity into one's life. Select the desired dimension and incorporate imagery or text that conveys financial prosperity. It could take the form of a significant monetary symbol or embody opulence through high-end concepts such as an exquisite property or fine jewelry.

Developing the vision board itself holds significant value within the visualization process. As you construct your board, concentrate on cultivating sensations of contentment, joy, and appreciation. Envisage yourself already attaining all the items you are affixing onto the board. Once you have completed the task, kindly place it in a location where it remains visible to you on a daily basis.

Technique for Visualizing Wealth #3: Envelop Yourself with a Prosperous Atmosphere.

Another effective technique entails immersing oneself in an environment abundant with financial resources. There is no need for you to attire yourself in tattered garments solely due to financial constraints. Furthermore, you need not vacate your residence in a dilapidated state due to a lack of motivation to enhance its appearance.

Transform your residence into a dwelling that exudes the ambiance of a high-achiever's abode. Moreover, I am not suggesting obtaining a loan and acquiring an assortment of home decorations. I kindly request that you adopt the mindset of an individual who has already achieved success.

Do not associate with individuals who continuously express dissatisfaction regarding their insufficient resources. Seek out individuals who possess a deep sense of satisfaction in their lives, and prioritize engaging in meaningful interactions with them.

These monetary visualization techniques possess the potential to greatly assist you, provided that you afford them an opportunity. The outcomes of your visualization may not always manifest in monetary terms. They can manifest as either an opportunity or an individual. Expand your perception and discern beyond the readily apparent and observable.

Tenets Of Effective Visualization

Set your intention

Visualization without establishing a deliberate objective is akin to possessing a high-end vehicle devoid of any means to propel it forward. The practice of employing mental imagery can serve as a doorway towards cultivating an elevated state of consciousness and unlocking one's innate spiritual capacities. It enables the practice of meditation, facilitating healing, facilitating communication, and offering a multitude of other possibilities. Lacking deliberate intent, one is unable to manifest their aspirations into tangible existence. Therefore, visualization is not effective for you.

Kindly refer to a few of these illustrations. Your objective is to cultivate a sense of positive energy and rejuvenate your spirit, mind, and body following a tiring and busy day. When envisioning without deliberate volition, your energies will not manifest into abundant recuperation. You will struggle to fully engage with positive energy. Your aims consist of investigating alternate realms or establishing a connection with your higher being, consequently employing visualization techniques to transport your physical being to such a state.

Your primary objective should be to achieve mental clarity, focusing on visualizing and fulfilling your intentions through the power of your mind's perception. You may observe that the absence of intention renders visualization devoid of purpose. However, this principle applies universally to every aspect of life, does it not? Every act that you undertake necessitates the volition to carry it out.

Nevertheless, within the realm of spirituality, its potency is undeniably formidable. Within the realm of your corporeal existence, you possess the capacity to freely manifest your desires by merely enacting corresponding physical actions. In matters of spirituality, one has the capacity to activate all aspects through the power of thought. Your thoughts manifest into reality and stimulate your physical existence to initiate action.

Ideas possess potent energies, and when coupled with intense and affirmative emotions, these ideas have the potential to materialize one's innermost aspirations. The intention has the potential to serve as the catalyst for unparalleled prosperity in your esteemed automobile. Intention can change anything.

Please rise and attempt to reach your toes (while some individuals may be capable, others may not be able to achieve the same). Therefore, if you are unable to touch them on your first attempt. On this occasion, I encourage you to perform the task once more with confidence and the belief in your abilities. Rest assured, you possess the capability to accomplish anything you set your mind to. Take decisive action now! Ideally, you have managed to avoid exerting excessive physical effort. I am curious to know the extent of your progress on this subsequent attempt. Indeed, the profound impact of intention is transformative in every aspect.

An ordinary observation such as strolling in the park cannot be actualized. Why? Due to the absence of your elevated consciousness in the realm of imagination. It can be referred to as indulging in fanciful thoughts. Consequently, it will not elicit a return to the individual.

If one harbors a profound mental image of acquiring a new residence, the likelihood of this materializing in reality is significantly heightened. It is imperative to engage in the practice of intentional visualization, with a particular emphasis on cultivating a resolute and unwavering intention. Frequently visualize the desired outcome and conduct yourself as though you have already attained ownership of the house, with the anticipation of imminent possession. It serves as a driving force that compels you to strive for your aspirations, thereby propelling you to undertake deliberate actions aligned with those aspirations.

Additionally, it establishes a cognitive framework for materializing and reestablishing one's existence, subsequently shaping both the present and future. And once it has reached sufficient strength, you possess the ability to transform your imaginative ideas into tangible manifestations.

Furthermore, your inner being will assist you in materializing your existence in alignment with the blueprint of your life. There's a problem, though. Consider the potential influence of one's intentions and the determination to genuinely accomplish a goal. You have envisioned linking with your ideal life partner, whose compatibility surpasses all realms, and you possess the ability to direct your intent towards manifesting their physical presence in your life. One can partake in the overwhelming joy and profound love that you both mutually cherish. Nonetheless, should any obstacles impede your intention, a significant impediment may arise in manifesting a compatible partner. For instance, you may harbor uncertainties regarding the feasibility of encountering an individual of such nature, or even questioning their very existence.

One may experience uncertainty regarding their readiness, doubts about deserving love, or concerns about making time for a new partner in light of their career obligations. All of these ideas and similar ones are diametrically opposed to your firm determination to encounter your ideal partner in life. One would engage in the practice of visualizing oneself returning home late from work, thereby depriving oneself of the opportunity to engage in meaningful interactions with one's significant other.

Any form of negative energy or detrimental thought patterns can serve as obstacles on your path to achieving success. The universe possesses awareness of your desires and acts accordingly. This phenomenon arises from your innate connection with the universe, which possesses a comprehensive understanding of your knowledge and endeavors to grant your deepest aspirations. Ensure that your visualization and intention are of utmost purity - they should be concentrated with untainted cognition and formidable emotional force channeled towards a singular objective. Subsequently, the extent of obstructive interference is mitigated. Adopt a mindset that promotes creativity while engaging in visualization with a firm sense of purpose.

You possess the ultimate authority as the creator, enabling you to exercise unrestricted discretion in your actions. The intention serves as the primary driving force in the process of visualization. During the practice of visualization, it is important to bear in mind that the imagery presented is generated by one's intention and cannot be independently created.

It is imperative to engage in consistent communication with one's higher self by establishing and adhering to the utmost level of intention. The significance lies in the intention underlying the process of healing, envisioning love, and setting goals. It is critical, given the circumstances, for the ethereal realm to be made aware of your desires for communication, and perhaps even more significantly, your preferences in terms of restricting unsolicited participation during such interactions, such as preventing any random spirit from joining the conversation. While every form of life on Earth holds significance, a primary factor behind humanity's domination of the planet is the elevated stage of spiritual advancement we possess, which continuously compels us to pursue growth. A resolute determination or unwavering resolve to bring about desired outcomes. Thus, we distinguish ourselves from animals in this manner.

Visualize Clearly

Taking mastery over your visualization is of utmost significance. As I delineated earlier, one can envision perceiving via a vibrant LCD television display. Certain individuals may possess the ability to perceive vibrant imagery, while others are limited to perceiving visualizations solely rendered in black and white. It is acceptable if a similar situation occurs to you as well. Ensure that you possess profound emotions that you are presently encountering during this process of visualization.

Simply cultivate a profound emotional response within yourself and endeavor to visualize with utmost clarity. Visualization is undeniably crucial, as it directly influences the manifestation of desired outcomes. The level of clarity attained through visualizing accurately enhances the likelihood of achieving one's goals. Develop vivid mental imagery and simultaneously incorporate affirmations for enhanced effect. The aforementioned affirmations encompass a wide range of intentions, such as expressing one's desires for accomplishment and aspirations for certain destinations. These visualizations and affirmations have the capacity to alter one's mindset. One may record their desires and aspirations in a personal journal and subsequently mentally envision them with precision, mirroring the exact manner in which they were inscribed.

Systematic Approaches of Employing Creative Visualization

While creative visualization possesses the potential to bring about transformative changes in one's life, its efficacy rests solely on the ability to apply it strategically and engage in deliberate practice. This can be a challenging task, particularly because influencing the mind or accessing its incredible potential can be quite difficult.

Various individuals incorporate creative visualization into their lives using diverse methods. The successful achievement of a goal is contingent upon the manner in which visualization techniques are employed. As previously noted, that is not always a straightforward task.

Fortunately, presented below are a handful of efficient strategies that can be employed to successfully integrate creative visualization into one's personal and professional endeavors.

Firstly, establish your objective

When establishing specific objectives, determine something that you desire to possess, regardless of its nature or magnitude. This could encompass a residential property, employment opportunity, interpersonal connection, or marital union. Nonetheless, I would kindly suggest considering these objectives. If you are new to the practice of creative visualization, it is advisable to select goals that are easily relatable and feasible for you to develop belief in.

By this, I am referring to objectives that you perceive as being attainable within a short timeframe. This approach will assist you in circumventing any adverse opposition that you may encounter, thereby enabling you to fully optimize the experience of success while practicing the art of creative visualization.

Allocate a minimum of 15 minutes per day to engage in envisioning the predetermined objectives; establishing this practice as a regular occurrence is highly advisable. You have the autonomy to determine the extent of time you wish to dedicate to this endeavor and achieve a consistent level of proficiency. Ensure that you select a location that is devoid of any disturbances as your designated area for visualization.

Second Step: Develop a Precise Concept or Visual Representation

Visualize or conceptualize the item or condition with utmost precision, directing your thoughts towards the exact manner in which you desire it to exist. It is crucial for you to adopt a present tense perspective, considering it as already existing in the desired manner.

Envision yourself immersed in a desired context, meticulously incorporating numerous intricate particulars. Repeatedly, imagine possessing the conceptual representation you have already constructed. It's a mental trick. In the process of visualization, one mentally conceptualizes the possession of a particular item.

If the need arises, you may also produce a tangible representation. The subconscious mind is incapable of discerning the boundary between imagination and reality. It will consistently behave in accordance with the images you have portrayed, both in your absence and in real-life scenarios.

Step #3: Prioritize Regular and Consistent Attention on the Matter

On numerous occasions, summon the mental imagery within your consciousness, both during meditative states and in the course of your daily activities. Through engaging in this practice, you will become acclimated to this. Over time, it becomes an integral aspect of your life. It increasingly manifests as a tangible actuality for you.

By maintaining a diligent and composed perspective, directing your attention towards its radiance, while also refraining from overwhelming determination and unnecessary exertion, you will succeed in attaining your objectives. As this negative sentiment is likely to impede your visualization capabilities, endeavor to make the experience tangible and enjoyable. Envision the envisioned outcomes once you successfully attain these objectives.

Step #4: Infuse it with a sense of positivity

It is imperative to maintain an unwavering focus on your objective while simultaneously cultivating a positive mindset towards it. Endeavor to construct robust, affirmative, and uplifting affirmations for personal use. Utilize phrases such as, "It is present, its arrival is imminent, and similar expressions." Visualize yourself

156

attaining your objectives or reaping the benefits they entail.

Whilst employing affirmations, it is advisable to temporarily set aside any reservations or skepticism one may hold towards their efficacy. Engage in the process of familiarizing yourself with the notion that your aspirations and visions are decidedly feasible and tangible.

Establish a consistent practice of engaging with this procedure until you successfully attain your objectives. It is imperative to bear in mind that goals often undergo changes before they become perceptible. This is an inherent component of the human journey towards evolution and development.

It is advisable to refrain from prolonging it beyond the amount of energy that you possess for it. This is due to the potential loss of interest that may occur. In the event of such an occurrence, there is an inevitable diminishment of one's inclination towards any objective.

Reaching a juncture where objectives shift, it is imperative to firmly recognize within oneself that the concentration has shifted away from a particular goal. Cease that cycle and initiate a fresh cycle to mitigate any perplexity or sense of inadequacy as it merely denotes a transition.

Reward is always important. Once you have accomplished any objective, it is important to deliberately acknowledge to yourself that the goal has been accomplished with certainty. Frequently, we attain the things we have been yearning for or envisioning, only to disregard their attainment as an accomplishment. Endeavor to express gratitude and acknowledge your efforts by offering commendation to yourself, while simultaneously expressing appreciation to the cosmos for manifesting your desires.

www.ingramcontent.com/pod-product-compliance
Lightning Source LLC
Chambersburg PA
CBHW071131050326
40690CB00008B/1422